AUSTRALIA'S REMARKABLE WILDLIFE

JOHN LESLEY

PLATYPUS

REDBACK publishing

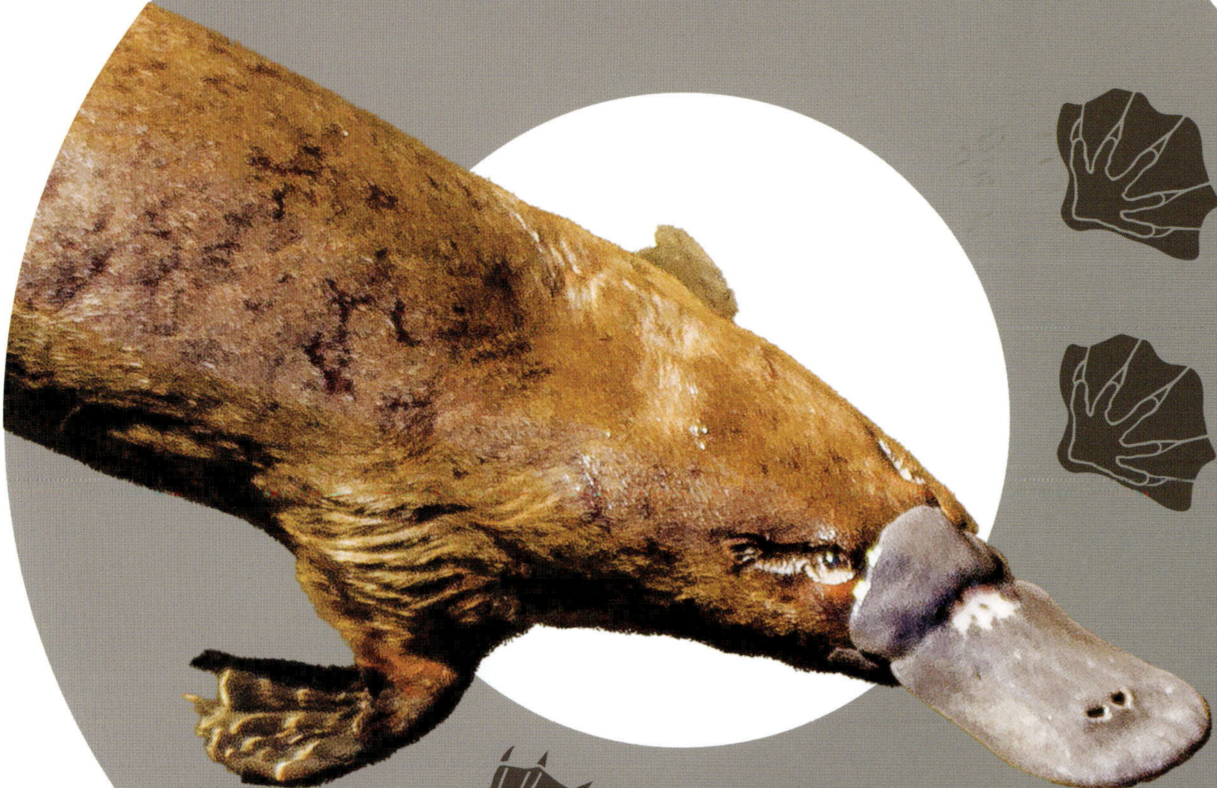

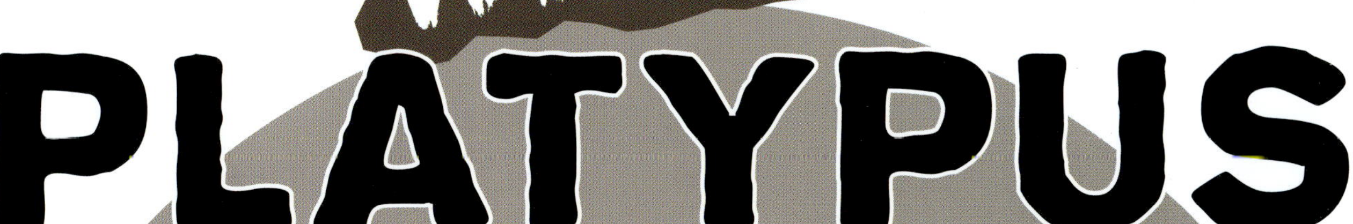

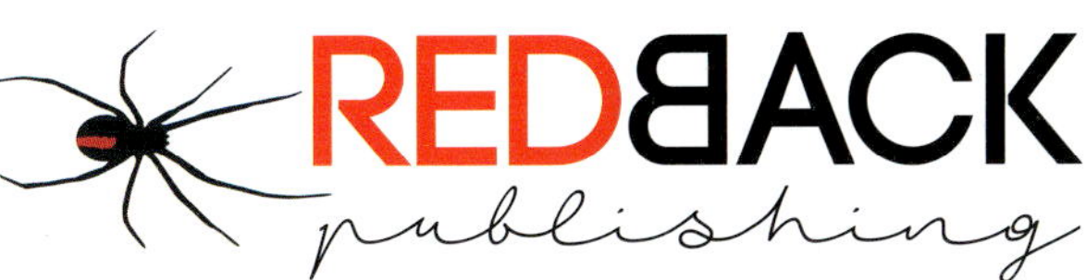

First Published 2025 by
Redback Publishing
Suite 6, 13a Narabang Way,
Belrose NSW 2085
Australia

www.redbackpublishing.com
orders@redbackpublishing.com

ISBN 978-1-761400-21-6 PBK

Author: John Lesley
Editor: Caroline Thomas
Design: Redback Publishing

Original illustrations © Redback Publishing 2025
Originated by Redback Publishing

A catalogue record for this book is available from the National Library of Australia

Printed and bound in Malaysia

Acknowledgements
Abbreviations: l—left, r—right, b—bottom, t—top, c—centre, m—middle
We would like to thank the following for permission to reproduce photographs: (Images © shutterstock)
p5tr Frederick Polydore Nodder, CC0, via Wikimedia Commons, p5bl User Magnus Manske on en.wikipedia, Public domain, via Wikimedia Commons, p6tl TwoWings, CC BY-SA 3.0 (https://creativecommons.org/licenses/by-sa/3.0), via Wikimedia Commons, p9tr Zoological Society of London.; Zoological Society of London., Public domain, via Wikimedia Commons, p8tr Steven Penton from Bakers Beach, Tasmania Australia, CC BY 2.0 (https://creativecommons.org/licenses/by/2.0), via Wikimedia Commons, p12br Vcby, CC BY-SA 4.0 (https://creativecommons.org/licenses/by-sa/4.0), via Wikimedia Commons, p15br Tentotwo, CC BY-SA 3.0 (https://creativecommons.org/licenses/by-sa/3.0), via Wikimedia Commons, p24ml Photodigitaal.nl, p30cr I Am birdsaspoetry.com from Melbourne, Australia, CC BY 2.0 (https://creativecommons.org/licenses/by/2.0), via Wikimedia Commons

CONTENTS

WHAT IS A PLATYPUS?

Is a platypus a duck, a mammal, a reptile or some strange combination of all of them? Ridiculous as this question sounds today, it was a serious consideration when the European colonists first caught a platypus and had a good look at it.

One Australian Indigenous origin story tells us that the platypus is the result of a mating between a duck and a water rat, a similar idea to that held by the first colonists who saw it.

4K UHD 3...2...1...0...1...2...3 00:35:02

SCIENTIFIC INVESTIGATION

In 1798, Governor Hunter sent a platypus skin and a drawing of the animal back to the British Museum for the scientists there to try to work out what sort of animal it was. After having a good look, and trying to make sure that the skin was not just a collection of different animal skins all sewn together as a joke, the naturalist, George Shaw, declared that it was indeed a real animal. He wrote that, *"it naturally excites the idea of some deceptive preparation by artificial means."*

George Shaw

MONOTREMES

Both platypuses and echidnas are the only two examples left alive on Earth of the rare group of mammals called monotremes. Eastern Australia is the only place on Earth where the rare platypus still exists.

Monotremes are a very ancient type of mammal, and they have one surprising feature. They all lay eggs!

TYPE OF ANIMAL

The platypus is a monotreme mammal, which means it has these characteristics:

The adult platypus is covered in fur.

The female lays eggs.

The platypus feeds its babies on milk from the mother's body.

The echidna and platypus both have the lowest body temperatures of any mammal that is not hibernating. This is because they cannot control their temperature the way marsupials and placental mammals do, suggesting a connection with very distant reptilian ancestors which were 'cold-blooded'.

Like their reptilian ancestors, the platypus and the echidna have legs that stick out sideways from the body, instead of pointing downwards.

PLATYPUS BASIC FACTS

SCIENTIFIC NAME

The scientific name for the platypus is *Ornithorhynchus anatinus*, which means having a nose like a duck's bill. The common name, platypus, means 'flat-footed'.

SIZE

The adult male platypus grows to about half a metre in length, and it weighs around two kilograms. The female is a little smaller.

SHAPE

The platypus has a streamlined body shape, with a snout that is shaped like a duck's bill. The tail is broad and flat. The feet have webbing between the claws for swimming.

Ornithorhynchus anatinus, the scientific name for the platypus, means having a nose like a duck's bill

00:35:02

COLOUR

The dense fur is dark brown on the back, and a lighter colour on the underside. The furry coat has two layers, and they keep the platypus skin dry under water. There is a small patch of yellow fur near each eye.

CONSERVATION STATUS

The IUCN Red List of Threatened Species records the platypus as 'Near Threatened' with its population numbers decreasing.

WHAT IS THE PLURAL OF PLATYPUS?

platypi.............................. ✗
platypuses...................... ✓
platypusses..................... ✗

THE PLATYPUS BODY

ADAPTATIONS

An adaptation can be either a change in the body, or a new type of behaviour that animals have developed to allow them to survive better in their environment.

An adaptation may be the result of a change in the animal's DNA in its genes, producing some helpful feature. This change can then be passed to their offspring.

When an animal learns a new behaviour that makes it more successful, it then passes this behaviour to its offspring through learning rather than by inheritance through its DNA and genes.

UHD

00:35:02

CLAWS

The strong claws are used to dig a burrow beside the water. When digging or when walking on land, the webbing between the claws is pulled backwards so it does not get in the way or become damaged.

VENOM

The males have a venomous spur on both of their back legs. They use the venom to fight off other males or predators.

SWIMMING

The platypus has a streamlined body so it can move swiftly through the water. Its thick tail is used as a rudder in the water. The webbed feet are used as paddles, and the water-repellent fur stops the skin getting wet when swimming.

THE BILL

The platypus has a leathery bill which is very sensitive and used to find food in the mud under the water. The bill can sense tiny electromagnetic changes in the water, caused when shrimps and other aquatic wildlife move around. Since the bill is so sensitive, the platypus can close its eyes when searching for food under water.

MILK

Like all other mammals, the female platypus produces milk to feed the babies.

VENOMOUS!

VENOMOUS MAMMALS

Although there are a few other mammals that are poisonous, they either have poisonous saliva, or they find poisons from the environment and spread them onto their bodies to deter predators from trying to eat them. The platypus is different because it has special venom glands and it inserts its venom into another animal. This is the same sort of adaptation that is found in the reptiles that are the platypus's distant relatives.

SPURS

The shy and extremely cute platypus is venomous. The male has a sharp spur on each of its back legs. Connected to the spur is a sac of venom. It uses this to protect itself by injecting the venom into any animal that threatens it. It will also attack another male during the mating season. The venom can kill small animals and is painful for a human. The platypus moves its back legs together against a predator, another male or a human hand, and forcefully jabs the spines and venom into it.

4K UHD
:35:02

PLATYPUS HABITATS

The platypus lives in clean, freshwater streams and lakes. It builds a burrow nearby with an entrance that is sometimes placed under the water. This keeps the platypus safe from most of its predators.

The platypus cannot survive in any sort of polluted water or in estuaries where there is salty, tidal water. Any pollutants that kill the crustaceans, insects and other water life will force a platypus to try to find somewhere else to live. If it cannot, then it will die from starvation or from heat exhaustion if it has to leave the water for an extended period of time.

Monotremes cannot control their body temperatures as well as placental or marsupial mammals do. Because of this, they cannot live in very hot regions, where they get overheated.

Platypuses live in rainforests, open forests and mountain regions. They cannot live in deserts or in frozen alpine regions, as they need access to water, which is where they find their food.

Rivers and creeks where cattle drink are no longer places where a platypus can survive. The stirring up of silt, the reduction of aquatic life, the trampling of the banks and the pollution from cattle manure make such locations unsuitable for platypuses.

Platypuses live in the southern and eastern parts of Australia, in Tasmania, Victoria and eastern New South Wales and Queensland. The platypuses on Kangaroo Island were introduced there as a conservation activity in the early 1900s.

PLATYPUS LIFE CYCLE

Apart from its unusual bill, the most remarkable feature of the platypus is that it lays eggs.

MATING

Adult platypuses live alone except when they come to together for mating, or when the female is looking after the babies. The male and female are ready to breed at about two years old. After mating, the female starts to build a nursery burrow, lining it with leaves and ferns.

LEAVING THE BURROW

After a few months, the baby platypuses leave the nest and look after themselves. A platypus may live for around ten years in the wild, but much longer in a zoo where it does not have predators and where there is always food and veterinary care.

LAYING THE EGGS

About three weeks after mating, the female produces from one to three tiny eggs that are less than two centimetres long. She does not have a pouch to put them in, but she curls her thick tail around them.

HATCHING

The eggs hatch after about ten days and begin to feed on the milk that the mother produces from special patches on her body. After hatching, the babies are just called baby platypuses. There was a short period when they were called puggles, but this name is now reserved just for baby echidnas. The term 'joey' is only used for baby marsupials and is not used for monotremes.

PLATYPUS ANCESTORS

60 MILLION YEARS AGO

The two monotremes alive today, the platypus and echidna, both descend from a single ancestor that lived about sixty million years ago. This is around the time that a meteor fell to Earth and probably resulted in the destruction of the dinosaurs. An outcome of this terrible event was that the small mammals alive at the same time as dinosaurs then had a better chance of spreading and evolving into the thousands of mammal species that are alive today, including the platypus.

At this time, Australia was a part of the ancient continent Gondwana, which also included the land that later separated into Africa, South America, Antarctica and India.

Fossils of ancient platypuses shows that some of them had teeth, and they were much bigger than they are today.

10,000 YEARS AGO

Before ten thousand years ago, Australia and Tasmania were all one mass of land. Sea levels were lower than they are today, and this allowed animals to move between areas that are now isolated from each other by seas and oceans, but which were then dry land.

As ice at the Poles melted around ten thousand years ago, the sea levels rose. This resulted in animals, such as platypuses, becoming isolated as water surrounded Australia and separated Tasmania.

PLATYPUS FOOD

INVERTEBRATES

Platypuses like to eat crustaceans, fish, worms and insects. They catch them in the water and in the mud at the bottom of a lake or stream. As they do not have teeth, platypuses take gravel into their mouth and use it to grind up their food by pushing the food and gravel against hard spots inside the mouth.

BILL

The bill is vital for enabling the platypus to find its food. The bill is very sensitive and has lots of receptors that help it locate little invertebrates that are good to eat. A platypus closes its eyes, ears and nostrils as it goes under the water, needing only its bill to find what it wants.

THREATS TO THE PLATYPUS

CLEAN ENVIRONMENT

Platypuses need clean water and quiet surroundings to survive. When people start building or farming nearby, the future survival of the platypus is under threat.

PREDATORS

Dingoes, snakes, eagles, feral dogs and foxes all like to eat platypuses and their babies.

PROTECTION

The platypus is a protected animal throughout Australia. This means they must not be harmed, moved or kept as pets. People who find an injured platypus should contact local wildlife services and take great care not to touch it. A sick or injured platypus may still be able to use its venomous spur to inflict a painful wound.

PEOPLE AND THE PLATYPUS

CLIMATE CHANGE

Climate change is contributing to rising summer temperatures, and what appears to be an increase in the number and severity of weather events such as flooding, droughts and storms. Unusual flooding destroys burrows and drowns baby platypuses. Droughts lead to streams drying up and the invertebrate wildlife dying. Without their food source in the water, platypuses will not be able to survive.

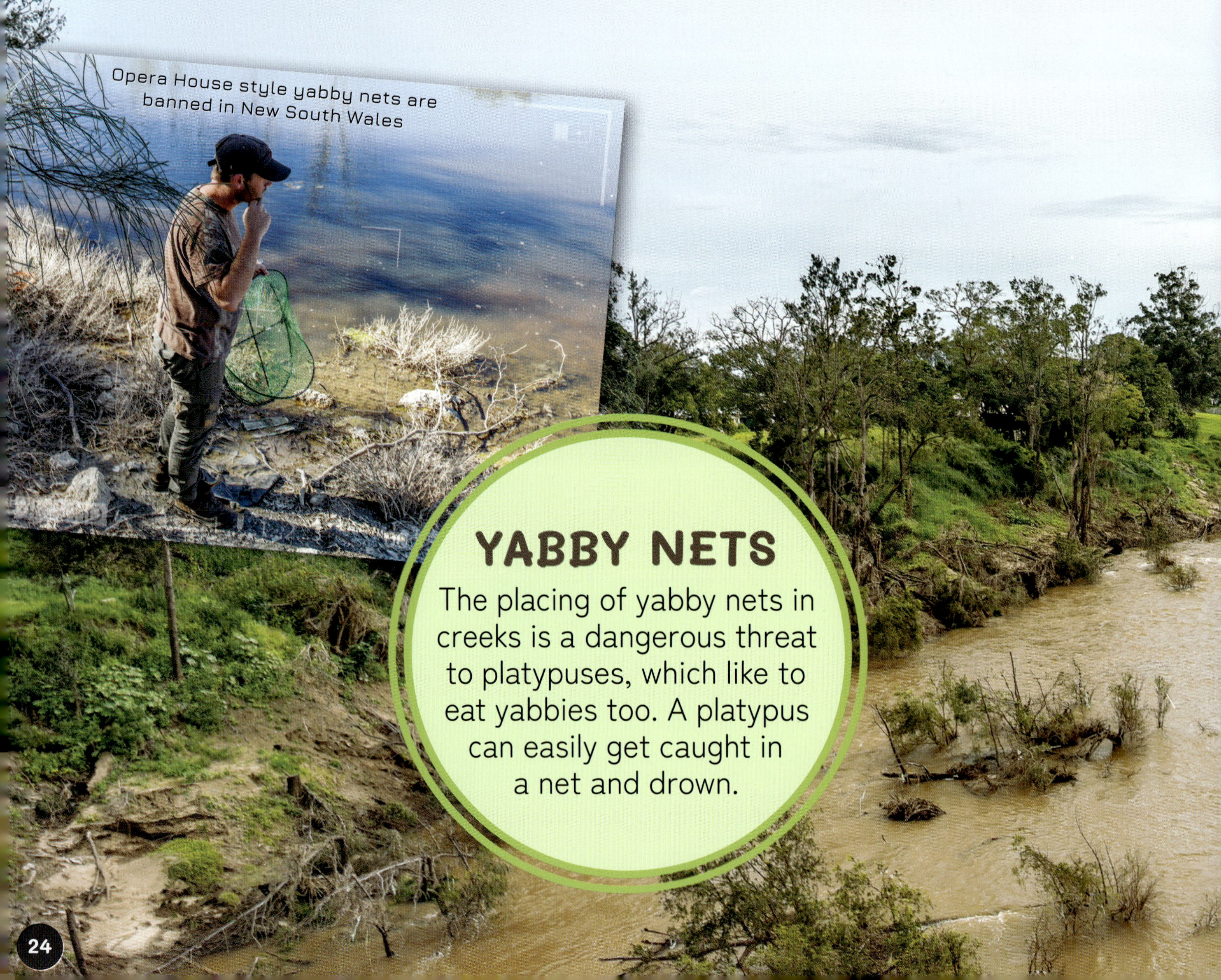

Opera House style yabby nets are banned in New South Wales

YABBY NETS

The placing of yabby nets in creeks is a dangerous threat to platypuses, which like to eat yabbies too. A platypus can easily get caught in a net and drown.

HUMAN ACTIVITIES

The human population of Australia is growing all the time. People need more space for their homes, roads and towns, and this means that less natural space is left for wildlife. When a new housing or factory development is built in a natural bushland area, the stormwater runoff from roads and roofs is often sent through drains into the local waterway. This runoff contains pollutants that damage the aquatic wildlife, not only near the development but further downstream as well. This makes the habitat unsuitable for platypuses.

IUCN RED LIST

The IUCN Red List of Threatened Species lists living things from around the world. The platypus is listed as NT Near Threatened.

WHERE TO SEE A PLATYPUS

IN THE WILD

The platypus is a very shy creature and seeing one in the wild is a rarity. They will hear you coming from a distance away and can probably also feel vibrations in the ground as you stomp through the bush. Long before you reach the place where they have been feeding, the platypus will have retreated into its burrow and be in hiding. Never take a dog with you if you suspect there might be a platypus nearby, as this is a certain way to ensure that you never get to see one.

ZOOS

Visiting a zoo in Australia is the easiest and surest way to see a platypus. Zoos arrange the exhibit lighting so that the platypus, which usually only comes out to feed at night, can be seen during the daytime by visitors.

SORTING ANIMALS INTO GROUPS

Biologists divide all living things around the world into groups. They call this process classification.

Here are the basic groups that describe all animals with backbones:

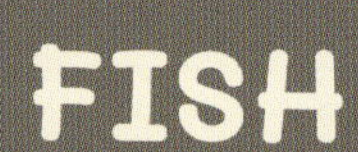

FISH

Examples are sharks and goldfish.

MAMMALS

Examples are dingoes and possums.

REPTILES

Examples are lizards and snakes.

BIRDS

Examples are emus and penguins.

AMPHIBIANS

Examples are frogs and salamanders.

Mammals are further divided into three main groups:

MONOTREME MAMMALS
Examples are echidnas and platypuses.

PLACENTAL MAMMALS
Examples are whales and humans.

MARSUPIAL MAMMALS
Examples are kangaroos and koalas.

HOMO SAPIENS

Humans have a scientific name and a position in the classification of animals. We are called *Homo sapiens*. These Latin words mean 'smart person'.

WATER RAT OR PLATYPUS?

WATER RAT OR PLATYPUS?

The native water rat is often mistaken for a platypus when people see it swimming in a lake or stream. Both animals are Australia's only two semi-aquatic mammals.

Here is how to tell the difference when you see them swimming:

PLATYPUS	WATER RAT (Rakali)
Broad, flat tail	Tail like a rope with a white tip
Large, flat bill	Blunt snout
None in Western Australia in the wild	Seen in the wild in southern Western Australia
No external ears	Ear flaps on top of head
No whiskers around mouth	Whiskers on snout
Rarely found in salty water	Swims in salty and fresh water

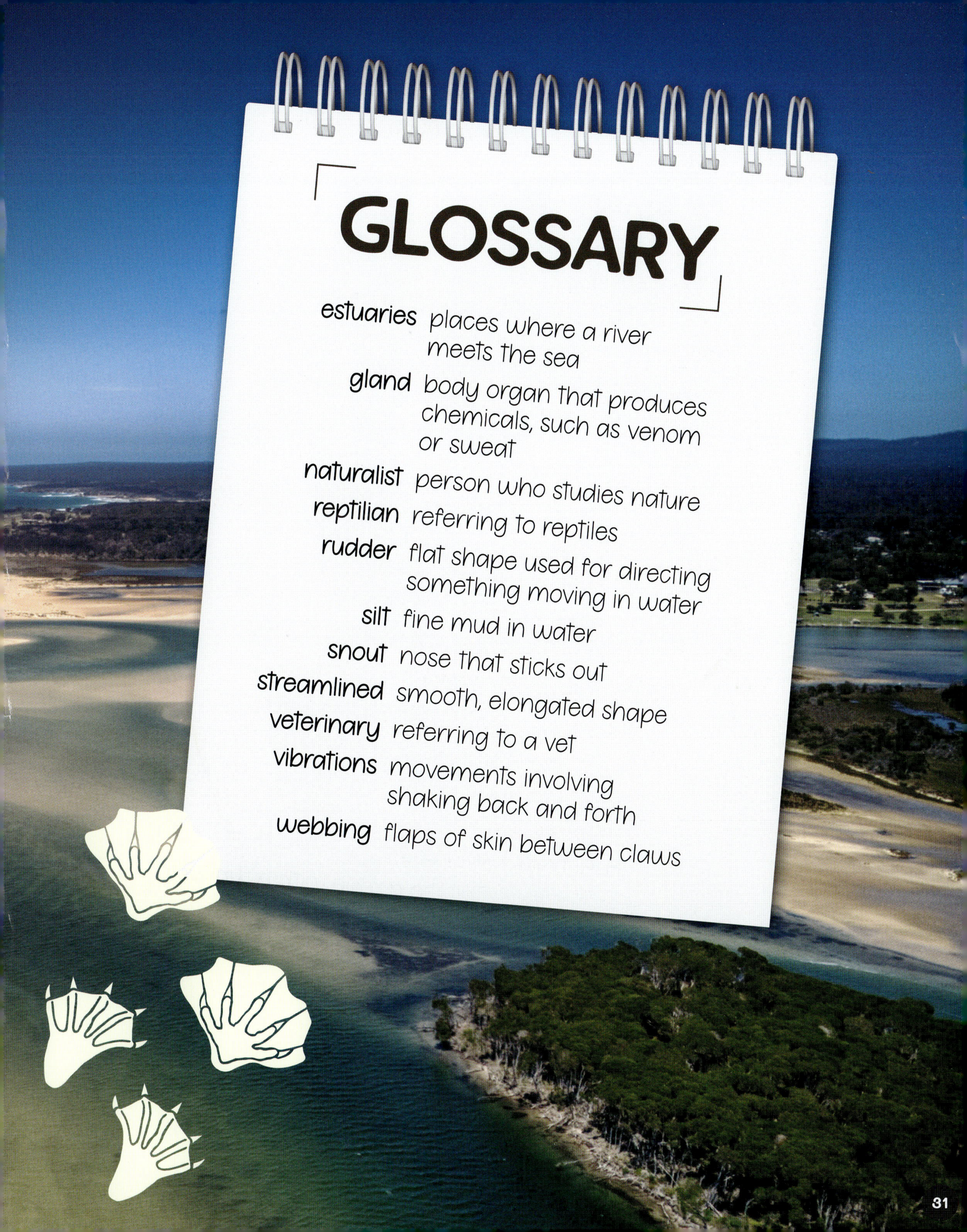

GLOSSARY

estuaries places where a river meets the sea

gland body organ that produces chemicals, such as venom or sweat

naturalist person who studies nature

reptilian referring to reptiles

rudder flat shape used for directing something moving in water

silt fine mud in water

snout nose that sticks out

streamlined smooth, elongated shape

veterinary referring to a vet

vibrations movements involving shaking back and forth

webbing flaps of skin between claws

INDEX